MAHATMA GANDHI

PEGASUS
www.pegasusforkids.com

© **B. Jain Publishers (P) Ltd.** All rights reserved. No part of this book may be reproduced, stored in a retrieval system or transmitted, in any form or by any means, mechanical, photocopying, recording or otherwise, without any prior written permission of the publisher.

Published by Kuldeep Jain for B. Jain Publishers (P) Ltd., D-157, Sector 63, Noida - 201307, U.P
Registered office: 1921/10, Chuna Mandi, Paharganj, New Delhi-110055

Printed in India

Contents

- 5   Who was Mahatma Gandhi?
- 6   Birth and Early Life
- 8   Gandhi as a Little Boy
- 14   Education and Marriage
- 19   Horrors of Africa
- 24   Fight for Indian Independence
- 35   Assassination
- 38   Death and Legacy
- 40   Gandhi and Secularism
- 45   Sabarmati Ashram
- 49   Gandhi and Untouchability
- 54   Gandhi's Views on Women
- 61   Timeline
- 65   Activities
- 67   Glossary

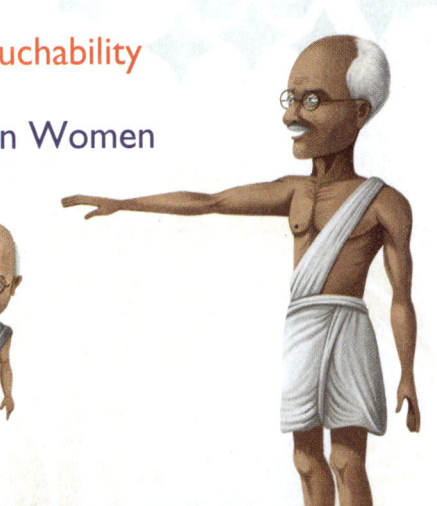

Who was Mahatma Gandhi?

Mahatma Gandhi, or Mohandas Karamchand Gandhi, was a prominent Indian political leader, lawyer, politician, social activist, and writer who campaigned for Indian independence. He was the primary leader of India's independence movement and also the architect of a form of non-violent civil disobedience that has influenced the entire world.

Mahatma Gandhi is internationally respected for his doctrine of non-violent protest, or satyagraha, to achieve political and social progress. He was assassinated in 1948, shortly after achieving his goal of Indian independence. In India, he is bestowed with the epithet 'Father of the Nation'.

Birth and Early Life

Mohandas Karamchand Gandhi, more commonly known as 'Mahatma' (meaning 'Great Soul'), was born in Porbandar, Gujarat, in North-West India, on October 2, 1869, into a Hindu merchant-class family. His father was the Chief Minister of Porbandar. While he was still a child, his mother infused in him a kind of devotion that taught tolerance, non-injury to living beings and following vegetarianism.

Gandhi was the youngest child of his father's fourth wife. His father—Karamchand Gandhi—was the Dewan (chief minister) of Porbandar, the capital of a small principality in western India (now called Gujarat) under British rule. He did not have much formal education. He was, however, an able administrator who knew how to steer his way between the impulsive princes, their long-suffering subjects, and the headstrong British political officers in power.

Gandhi's mother, Putlibai, was a religious lady and did not care much for finery or jewellery. She spent her time between her home and the temple, fasted frequently, and busied herself by nursing whenever there was a sickness in the family. Gandhi grew up in a home steeped in Vaishnavism (worship of Lord Vishnu) with a strong tinge of Jainism, a morally rigorous Indian religion whose chief tenets are non-violence and the belief that everything in the universe is eternal. So, he largely stood by ahimsa or non-injury to all living beings, vegetarianism and fasting for self-purification, and mutual tolerance between various creeds and sects.

7

Gandhi as a Little Boy

As a child, Gandhi was not bright at studies. However, he was extremely fond of reading books. Once he read the story of Shravana Kumar, a famous Indian mythological character. The story talks about how Shravana used to carry his old, blind parents in two baskets slung on a bamboo yoke. Gandhi was deeply touched by the story and Shravana's devotion to his old parents. He also wanted to be like Shravana Kumar and serve his parents.

One day, Gandhi saw a play depicting the life of King Harishchandra, who lost his kingdom and suffered miserably for truth. Gandhi was so deeply moved by this play that he was in tears. He decided never to steer from the path of truth and be ever truthful and honest like Harishchandra.

Gandhi used to be a timid boy in his childhood days. He was afraid to step in darkness even in his own house. He feared ghosts, thieves and snakes. A maid-servant in his household, Rambha, once said to Gandhi, "Why are you so much fearful? Remember Rama! Rama will always protect you. Fear never comes to him who remembers Rama."

Gandhi was deeply impressed by these words. He took to reciting the name of Rama. His faith in Rama increased as he grew up. He remembered God and dedicated all his work to him. Even when he died, his last words were: "Hey Rama!"

Gandhi's father, Karamchand Gandhi, was popularly known as Kaba Gandhi. In early years, he was the Dewan of Porbandar, following which he became the Dewan of Rajkot. During his stay in Rajkot, his Parsee and Muslim friends would often visit his house and discuss the good in their religions. Young Gandhi often sat by father's side, lending a keen ear to these discussions. These debates created in him a genuine love for all religions.

Once, the Inspector of schools came to visit the school where Gandhi was studying. He wanted to test the boys, so he dictated a few English words to them. Gandhi could not spell one of the words correctly. So, his teacher prompted him to copy that word from his neighbour's slate, but Gandhi refused to do so. He did not like to cheat anybody. The result was that all the students except Gandhi had spelt all the words correctly. The teacher scolded Gandhi after the class, which left a deep impact on his mind. However, deep inside him he knew that what he had done was right.

In those days, India was under the British rule. Once a boy told Gandhi, "Do you know why the British are so strong and why they can rule over us? It is because they eat meat. If we become meat-eaters, like them, we will be able to drive them out."

Gandhi was convinced by this argument. But everybody in Gandhi's family was strictly vegetarian; so he tried eating meat outside. He did not disclose this secret to anybody, yet he was averse to telling a lie and deceiving his parents. So, finally he decided not to touch meat again.

By this time, Gandhi had also taken to smoking cigarettes. For this he had to steal money and to incur debt. When the debt increased, he stole a piece of gold from one of the gold bracelets that his brother wore and paid off the debt.

But soon after that, his heart was filled with repentance and he resolved never to steal again. He wrote down a confession of his crime on a piece of paper and put it in the hands of his father, who was then sick. His father read the letter and without uttering a word, tore up the paper with a deep sigh. Gandhi was deeply hurt. Tears rolled down his cheeks. It was at that moment that he had realized the power of truth. From that day, telling the truth became a passion with him. He loved his father more and more.

Gandhi, from his childhood days, was highly conscious of his character. He guarded against spoiling it. Even a slight hint of blame towards him would bring tears from his eyes. He was very hardworking too.

Due to his shy and aloof nature, he never took part in any sport. He thought gymnastics and education had no relation. Gandhi as a boy was lean and thin. He was thinner than his siblings.

13

Education and Marriage

Born into a privileged stratum of society, Gandhi was fortunate to receive a comprehensive education, but proved to be a mediocre student. At that time, the educational facilities offered at Porbandar were very basic. In the primary school that Gandhi attended, the children wrote the alphabet in the dust with their fingers. Although Gandhi occasionally won prizes and scholarships at the local schools, his record was on the whole average. One of the term reports rated him as 'good at English, fair in Arithmetic and weak in Geography; conduct very good, bad handwriting.'

In May 1883, when Gandhi was 13 years of age, he was married to Kasturba Makhanji. The marriage was fixed through the arrangement of their respective parents, as was customary at that time.

After marriage, Gandhi began to keep watch on Kasturba's movements. Kasturba, on her part, did not like to take her husband's permission for going out. So Gandhi started growing jealous and put more restrictions on her. This led to some bitterness between them. Kasturba was 11 years old at the time of her marriage and was quite straightforward in following her own ideas.

Gandhi's love for his young wife knew no bounds. Even while he was in school, she would constantly haunt his

15

mind. At home, he kept talking to her till late in the night. So lost was he in his thoughts that he lost one year of school after marriage.

Till Gandhi turned 18, they stayed hardly for three years together. Since Kasturba was still a small girl, after every six months, her parents took her back home. This made Gandhi quite nervous.

When Gandhi entered Samaldas College at the University of Bombay, Kasturba bore him the first of their four sons, in 1888. Gandhi was unhappy at college. So, when he was offered the opportunity of furthering his studies overseas, at University College London, at the age of 18, he accepted the offer with eagerness. He left for overseas in September 1888.

In London, he was educated in law at the University College. In 1891, after having been admitted to the British bar, Gandhi returned to India and attempted to establish a law practice in Bombay, without much success. Two years later, an Indian firm with interests in South Africa retained him as a legal adviser in its office in Durban.

Horrors of Africa

When Gandhi arrived in Durban, he found himself treated as a member of an inferior race. He was appalled at the widespread denial of civil and political rights to Indian immigrants to South Africa. He at once fell into a struggle for elementary rights for Indians.

Although not yet enshrined in law, the system of 'apartheid' was very much prevalent in South Africa at the turn of the 20th century. Despite arriving on a year's contract, Gandhi spent the next 21 years living in South Africa, and fought against the injustice of racial segregation. On one occasion he was thrown out of a first class train compartment, despite having a valid 1st Class ticket. The racial bias experienced by his countrymen served as a catalyst for his later activism. As a result, he attempted to fight segregation at all levels.

He founded a political movement, known as the Natal Indian Congress, and developed his theoretical belief in non-violent civil protest, when he opposed the introduction of registration for all Indians, within South

Africa, through non-cooperation with the relevant civic authorities. Gandhi began to teach a policy of passive resistance to, and non-cooperation with, the South African authorities. Part of the inspiration for this policy came from the Russian writer Leo Tolstoy, whose influence on Gandhi was profound. Gandhi also acknowledged his debt to the teachings of Christ.

On his return to India in 1915, Gandhi developed his practice of non-violent civic disobedience still further. He raised awareness against the oppressive practices in Bihar in 1918, when he saw the local population oppressed largely by their British masters. He also encouraged oppressed villagers to improve their own circumstances by leading peaceful strikes and protests. His fame spread, and he became widely referred to as 'Mahatma' or 'Great Soul'.

Fight for Indian Independence

Indian nationalism may be divided into three distinct phases. In the first phase, the ideology of the moderates dominated the political scene. This was followed by the second phase in which leaders with extremist ideologies dominated. In the third phase of Indian nationalism, the most significant incident was the rise of Gandhi to power as the leader of various national movements. Under his spirited guidance, the movements of the country took shape.

In the year 1915, Gandhi returned to India, where he lent his support to the Home Rule Movement. He became the leader of the Indian National Congress, advocating a policy of non-violence and non-cooperation to achieve independence. His goal was to help poor farmers and labourers protest against oppressive taxation laws and discrimination. He struggled to wipe out poverty, liberate women and put an end to caste discrimination, with the ultimate objective of obtaining self-rule for India.

During World War I, in which Gandhi played an active role in organizing campaigns, he again advocated Satyagraha and launched his movement of non-violent resistance to Great Britain. In 1919, when the Parliament passed Rowlatt Acts, giving the Indian colonial authorities emergency powers to deal with so-called revolutionary activities, Satyagraha spread throughout India, gaining millions of followers. A demonstration against the Acts resulted in massacre of Indians at Amritsar by British soldiers.

In 1920, when the British government failed to make changes in this respect, Gandhi proclaimed an organized campaign of 'non-cooperation'. Indians in public offices resigned, government agencies such as courts of law were boycotted, and Indian children were withdrawn from government schools. Throughout India, streets were blocked by squatting Indians who refused to rise even when beaten by police. Gandhi was arrested, but the British were soon forced to release him.

1921, he was leading the Indian National Congress, and reorganizing the party's constitution around the principle of 'Swaraj', or complete political independence from the British. He also instigated a 'boycott' of British goods and institutions. It was due to his encouragement that mass civil disobedience took place. This led to his arrest, on March 10, 1922, for which he served two years, of a six-year prison sentence.

Gandhi launched the Civil Disobedience Movement in the year 1930. This was an important milestone in the history of Indian nationalism. The Indians learnt how the tenets like non-violence and passive resistance could be used to wage political battles. The programmes and policies adopted in the movements reflected his political ideologies of 'ahimsa' and 'satyagraha'.

On the historic day of March 12, 1930, Gandhi inaugurated the Civil Disobedience Movement by conducting the Dandi Salt March, where he broke the Salt Laws imposed by the British Government. Followed by an entourage of 78 followers, Gandhi embarked on his march from Sabarmati

Ashram to Dandi that is located on the shores of the Arabian Sea. On April 6, 1930, Gandhi, accompanied by 78 satyagrahis, violated the Salt Law by picking up a fistful of salt lying on the sea shore. They manually made salt on the shores of Dandi.

Dandi Salt March had an immense impact on the entire nation. Each and every corner of the country was gripped in a unique fervour of nationalism.

While the Non-Cooperation Movement was built on the lines of non-violence and non-cooperation, the essence of the Civil Disobedience Movement was defiance of the British laws. Through his leadership in the national movements, Gandhi played a crucial role in the unification of the country, awakening of the masses, and bringing politics within the arena of the common public.

During the first years of the Second World War, Gandhi's mission to achieve independence from Britain reached its zenith. He saw no reason why Indians should fight for British sovereignty in other parts of the world, when they were subjugated at home. This led to the worst instances of civil uprising under his direction, through his Quit India Movement. As a result, he was arrested again on August 9, 1942, and held for two years at the Aga Khan Palace in Pune. In February 1944, three months before his release, his wife Kasturba died in the same prison.

By 1944, the Indian struggle for independence was in its final stages. The British government agreed to give independence but on one condition that the two contending nationalist groups—the Muslim League and the Congress party—should resolve their differences. Gandhi stood steadfastly against the partition of India. The Muslims wanted a separate country. Ultimately, Gandhi had to yield to the demands, hoping that peace would be restored after the Muslim demand for separation had been satisfied. India and Pakistan became separate states when the British granted India its independence in 1947.

During the riots that followed the partition of India, Gandhi pleaded with the Hindus and Muslims to live together peacefully. Riots engulfed Calcutta (now Kolkata), one of the largest cities in India, and the Mahatma fasted until disturbances ceased.

Assassination

On January 30, 1948, whilst Gandhi was on his way to a prayer meeting at Birla House in Delhi, Nathuram Godse, a Hindu fanatic, managed to get close enough to him in the crowd to be able to shoot him three times in the chest, at point-blank range. The world was horrified by the death of a man nominated five times for the Nobel Peace Prize.

Godse, who had made no attempt to flee following the assassination, and his co-conspirator, Narayan Apte, were both imprisoned until their trial on November 8, 1949. They were convicted of Gandhi's killing, and both were executed, a week later, at Ambala Jail, on November 15, 1949. Gandhi was cremated as per Hindu rituals, and his ashes are interred at the Aga Khan's palace in Pune, the place his wife had also died.

Gandhi's death was regarded as an international catastrophe. His place in humanity was measured not in terms of the 20th century, but in terms of history. A period of mourning was set in the United Nations General Assembly, and condolences to India were expressed by all countries alike. Religious violence soon waned in India and Pakistan, and the teachings of Gandhi came to inspire non-violent movements elsewhere, notably in the U.S.A. under the civil rights leader Martin Luther King, Jr. and in South Africa under Nelson Mandela.

Death and Legacy

Even after his death, Gandhi's commitment to non-violence and his belief in simple living—making his own clothes, eating a vegetarian diet and keeping fasts for self-purification as well as a means of protest—have been a ray of hope for oppressed people throughout the world.

Although Gandhi was nominated for the Nobel Peace Prize five times, he never received it. In the year of his death, 1948, the prize was not awarded, the stated reason being that 'there was no suitable living candidate' that year.

Gandhi's life and teachings have inspired many liberationists of the 20th century, including Dr. Martin Luther King in the United States, Nelson Mandela and Steve Biko in South Africa, and Aung San Suu Kyi in Myanmar.

39

Gandhi and Secularism

Mahatma Gandhi was a keen student of all religions. Apart from his study of Hinduism, Buddhism and Jainism, he was an avid reader of Christian and Islamic scriptures as well. All forms of religion attracted Gandhi immensely, and through his thorough understanding of all, he successfully arrived at a composite understanding of religion and God as a whole.

This holistic understanding of man's spiritual quest led Gandhi to adopt and preach the theory of tolerance and mutual respect founded on non-violence.

Gandhi believed that God is one and he variously equated him to love and truth. The poor and the downtrodden were for Gandhi the living representatives of God on earth, and even a little work for the lessening of their troubles was a more pious act than performing a thousand rituals.

Gandhi read the scriptures and doctrines of all major world religions with great interest and finally arrived at a conclusion that they are all 'more or less' the same. They were all equal in their imperfection, the reason why Gandhi never foresaw a future where there will be a single religion preaching a single God.

Religious practices for Gandhi were equally vacuous if not meant for the general good and betterment of society. Leading a humble life with a strong belief in God was more of a religious duty for Gandhi than undertaking elaborate rituals. He put great stress on prayer, non-violence and celibacy as ways of spiritual enlightenment. He strongly believed that salvation was the ultimate goal of life.

Gandhi preached his ideals of secularism and religious tolerance across the length and breadth of the country. He showed his consolidation to the Muslim leaders through the support that Congress extended to the Khilafat Movement. Gandhi wrote extensively on the need of secularism in India and made speeches to the same effect all over the country. It was not the easiest of tasks for Gandhi.

Sabarmati Ashram

On his return from South Africa, Gandhi established his first ashram—Sabarmati Ashram—in India in the Kochrab area of Ahmedabad on May 25, 1915. The ashram was then shifted on June 17, 1917 to a piece of open land on the banks of River Sabarmati. Why this ashram was shifted had many reasons behind it. For instance, Gandhi wanted to do some experiments in farming, animal husbandry, cow breeding, Khadi and related constructive activities, for which he was in search of this kind of open land.

The Sabarmati Ashram, also known as the Harijan Ashram, was the home to Gandhi from 1917 until 1930 and served as one of the main centres of the Indian freedom struggle. Originally called the 'Satyagraha Ashram', reflecting the movement toward passive resistance launched by the Mahatma, the ashram became home to the ideology that set India free.

Sabarmati Ashram, named after the river on whose banks it is located, was created with a dual mission—to serve as an institution that would carry on a search for truth and a platform to bring together a group of workers committed to non-violence who would help secure freedom for India.

While at the ashram, Gandhi formed a school that focused on manual labour, agriculture and literacy to advance his efforts for self-sufficiency. It was also from here that on March 12, 1930, Gandhi launched the famous Dandi March, 241 miles from the ashram, with 78 companions in protest of the British Salt Law.

Over the years, the ashram became home to the ideology that set India free. It helped numerous other nations and people in their own battles against oppressive forces.

Today, the ashram serves as a source of inspiration and guidance, and stands as a monument to Gandhi's life mission.

Gandhi and Untouchability

According to Gandhi, the practice of untouchability is 'a leper wound in the whole body of Hindu politic'. He even regarded it as 'the hate-fullest expression of caste'. He made it his life's mission to wipe out untouchability and to uplift the downtrodden people. He preached that all human beings are equal and hence the Harijans too have a right for social life along with other caste groups.

Gandhi strongly believed in the four-fold division of the Hindu society into four 'varnas'. He regarded untouchables as shudras and not as the 'panchamas' or fifth varna or 'avarna'.

Hence, he sincerely felt the need for bringing about a basic change in the caste structure by uplifting the untouchables and not by abolishing the caste as such. He appealed to the common masses to realize the historical necessity of accommodating the 'Harijans' (the people who did lowly jobs like sweepers, washers of clothes, leatherworkers, etc.) by providing them a rightful place in society.

Gandhi had a lot of compassion for the Harijans. He once said, "I do not want to be reborn. But if I am to be born, I would like to be born an untouchable, so that I may share their sorrows and sufferings."

According to him, the practice of untouchability is a moral crime. He once said, "If untouchability is not wrong, then nothing in the world is wrong." He believed that a change of heart on the part of the Hindus was essential to enable the social and cultural assimilation of Harijans. He was deeply touched by their social distress and started a nationwide crusade.

51

Gandhi widely addressed various public meetings reposing doctrines of Harijan welfare. He led several processions of Harijans with other upper caste people and made them participate in the religious activities like performing 'poojas' (an act of worship) and singing of 'bhajans' (religious songs).

Gandhi believed that opportunities of education and the entry of Harijans would reduce social inequalities between them and high-caste Hindus. He launched movements for cleaning Harijan residential areas, for digging wells for them and for similar other beneficial things.

Gandhi served the 'Harijan Sevak Sangha' started by the social reformer Takkar Bapa in the year 1932. The Sangha was started for the religious and social welfare of the Harijans. The organization opened schools and dispensaries in various places, and also arranged for free educational facilities and scholarships for Harijan children.

From 1920 onwards, under the leadership of Gandhi, the Indian National Congress became committed to gain independence on the one hand and to remove untouchability on the other.

The Harijan Sevak Sangh, at a conference held in Bombay (now Mumbai), pledged that the right to use public roads, wells, etc. would be given legal recognition when the Swaraj Parliament met.

This pledge was stressed by Gandhi in 1932 when he said, "There could be no rest … until untouchability becomes a thing of the past."

The Harijan movement gained strength throughout the country. Gandhi went on an all-India tour to collect huge sums of money for the movement.

As a result of his sincere efforts and strong recommendations, untouchability was declared illegal under the Indian Constitution.

Gandhi's Views on Women

Women in Pre-Independence India

To understand the role that Gandhi played in improving the position of women in the Indian society, it is essential to look at women's status prevalent at that time. When Gandhi emerged on to the political scene of pre-independent India, social evils like child marriage and dowry system were rampant. Indian women had an average life span of only twenty-seven years. Death of women during childbirth was a common phenomenon. The percentage of women with basic education was as low as 2 percent. Women were considered to be inferior and subordinate to their male counterparts. The 'purdah' system was in full vogue in northern India. Unless accompanied by their male guardians, the women were not permitted to venture out on their own. Only a handful few could avail education and attend schools. It was in such a dismal situation that Gandhi began his social crusade that led to a major change in the status of women in the Indian society.

Gandhi's Protest against Social Evils

According to Gandhi, social reforms were essential for the restructuring of societal values that had so far dominated the Indian women. The custom of child marriage became a target of his criticism. In his opinion, child marriage was a source of physical degeneration as much as a moral evil. The system of dowry could not pass unnoticed from his

55

critical eyes. He defined dowry marriages as 'heartless'. In his opinion, girls should never marry men who demand dowry. As Gandhi believed that the basis of marriage is mutual love and respect, he encouraged people to enter into inter-communal marriages between the Harijans and Hindus.

Gandhi was extremely disturbed by the condition of the widows, particularly child widows. He put forth an earnest appeal to the young generation of the country to marry the widows. He was also quite hopeful about the fact that the widows could contribute a a great deal to the national issues if given a chance.

The system of 'purdah', or covering the face of women in front of males, also came under Gandhi's attacks and he questioned the very foundation of this practice. He left no stone unturned to restore the honour of women.

Gandhi's Perception of Women

Gandhi had a very noble perception of women, which was based on real life observations during his own life which was full of struggles. For Gandhi, women were not mere toys in the hands of men, neither their competitors. According to him, men and women are essentially endowed with the same spirit and abilities. Therefore, they share similar problems also. Women, in his view, were at par with men, one complementing the other.

According to Gandhi, education for women was the need of the time that would ensure their moral development and make them capable of occupying the same platform as that of men. In Gandhi's views, women could never be considered to be the weaker sex. In fact, women were embodiments of virtues like knowledge, humility, tolerance, sacrifice and faith. These qualities he thought were essential prerequisites for imbibing the virtue of satyagraha.

The capability of tolerating endless suffering can be witnessed only in women, according to the Mahatma. The doctrine of ahimsa as preached by Gandhi incorporates the virtue of suffering as was evident in the Indian women. Therefore, Gandhi visualized a critical role for women in establishing non-violence. He invoked the instances of ancient role models who were epitomes of Indian womanhood, like Draupadi, Savitri, Sita and Damayanti, to show that Indian women could never be feeble. Women had equal mental abilities as that of men and an equal right to freedom. To sum up in Gandhi's words, "The wife is not the husband's slave but his companion and his helpmate and an equal partner in all his joys and sorrows—as free as the husband to choose her own path."

Role of Women as Visualized by Gandhi

According to Gandhi, the role of women in the political, economic and social emancipation of the country was of extreme importance. He had immense faith in the capability of women to carry on a non-violent crusade. Under his guidance and leadership, women shouldered critical responsibilities in India's struggle for freedom. Women held public meetings, organized picketing of shops selling foreign alcohol and articles, sold Khadi and actively participated in national movements. They bravely faced the baton of the police and even went behind the bars.

Gandhi's urge to women to join India's struggle for independence was instrumental in transforming the outlook of women. Through their participation in the

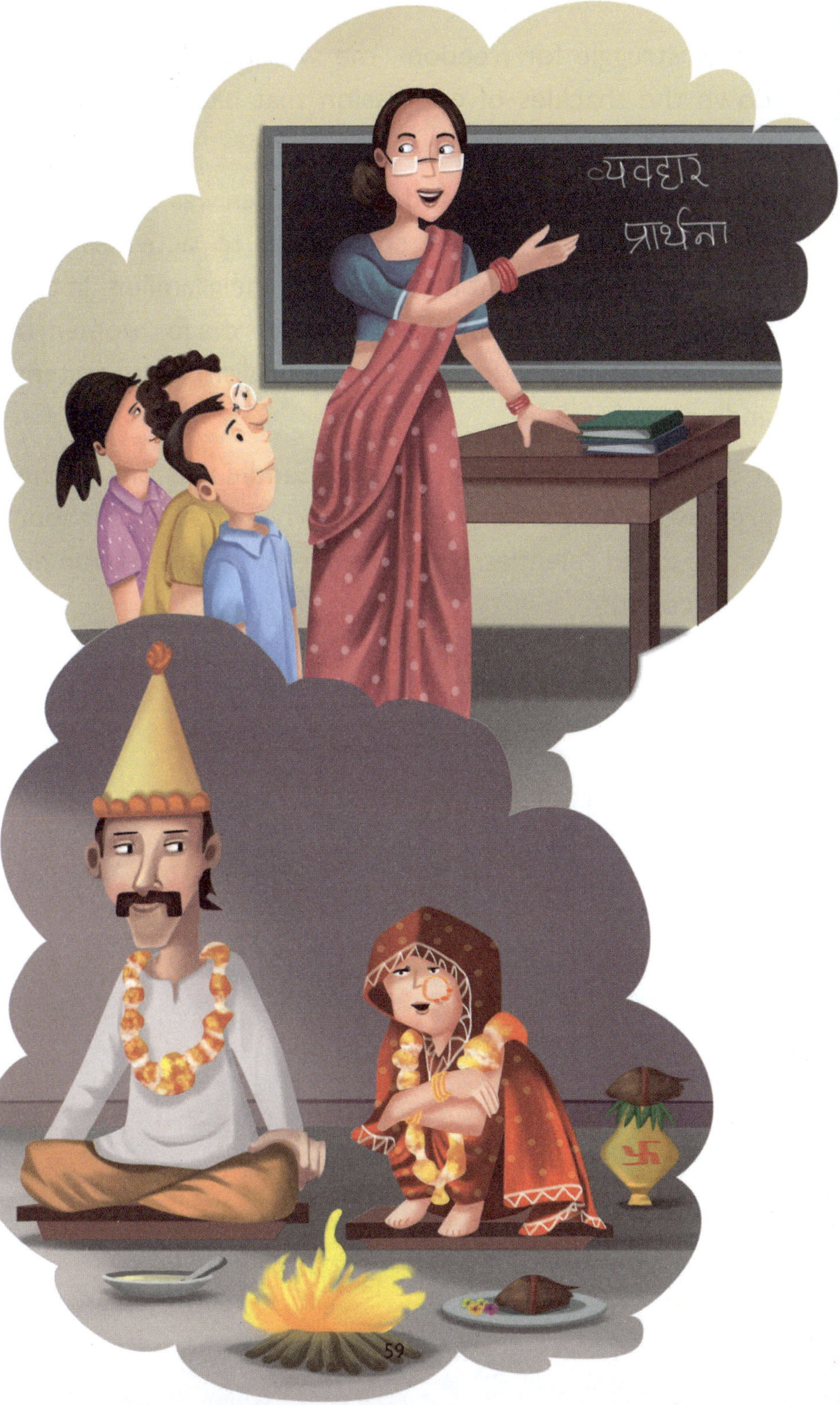
व्यवहार
प्रार्थना

Indian struggle for freedom, the women of India broke down the shackles of oppression that had bound them from time immemorial.

As far as the economic freedom of women was concerned, Gandhi felt that women could take to activities like spinning to supplement the income of their families. In the social realm, Gandhi envisaged a critical role for women in doing away with the forces of communalism, caste system and untouchability.

It can be said without doubt that Gandhi was one of the greatest advocates of women's liberty and all throughout his life toiled relentlessly to improve the status of women in his country.

- 1869 Gandhi is born on October 2, at Porbandar, Kathiawad, to Karamchand (Kaba) and Putlibai Gandhi

- 1876 He attends primary school in Rajkot, where his family moved

- 1876 He gets engaged to the daughter of Gokuldas Makanji, a merchant

- 1881 Gandhi enters high school in Rajkot

- 1883 He gets married to Kasturba

- 1885 His father dies at the age of 63

- 1887 Gandhi passes matriculation examination at Ahmedabad and enters Samaldas College, Bhavnagar, Kathiawad; he finds it difficult to concentrate in his studies

- 1888 Gandhi's first of the four sons is born

- 1891 He sails from Bombay to England to study law

- 1891 He returns to India in summer after being called to bar; begins practice of law in Bombay and Rajkot

- 1893 Gandhi sails for South Africa to become lawyer for an Indian firm

Timeline

- 1893 He finds himself subjected to all kinds of colour discrimination

- 1894 He prepares to return to India after completing law case, but is persuaded by Indian colony to remain in South Africa, do public work and earn a living as a lawyer.

- 1894 He organizes the Natal Indian Congress

- 1896 Gandhi comes back to India for six months to bring back his wife and two children to Natal

- 1901–1902 He travels extensively in India, attends the Indian National Congress meeting in Calcutta, and opens a law office in Bombay

- 1914 He leaves South Africa forever, sailing from Cape town to London with Kasturba and Kallenbach, and arriving just at the beginning of World War I

- 1915 He establishes the Satyagraha Ashram at Kochrab, near Ahmedabad, and soon admits an untouchable family; in 1917, he moves the ashram to a new site on Sabarmati River

- 1918 He leads a satyagraha campaign for peasants in Kheda

- 1919 Rowlatt Bills passed, and first all-India satyagraha campaign is conceived

- 1919 Gandhi organises nation-wide 'hartal' (suspension of activity for a day) against Rowlatt Bills

- 1920 He successfully urges resolution for a satyagraha campaign of non-cooperation at Muslim Conference in Allahabad and at Congress sessions in Calcutta and Nagpur

- 1921 The first shop for selling homespun (khadi) clothes opens in Bombay

  Gandhi gives up wearing shirt and cap, and resolves to wear only a loin-cloth in devotion to homespun cotton

- 1928 He moves compromise resolution at Congress session in Calcutta, calling for complete independence within one year, or else the beginning of another all-Indian satyagraha campaign

- 1929 He is arrested for burning foreign cloth in Calcutta

- 1930 He breaks salt law by picking salt up at seashore as the whole world watches

Timeline

- 1933 He begins weekly publication of 'Harijan' in place of 'Young India'

- 1933 Gandhi begins self-purification fast of 21 days against untouchability and is released from prison by government on the first day; he breaks his fast after 21 days at Poona

- 1933 He disbands Sabarmati ashram, which becomes the centre for removal of untouchability

    He embarks on a 10-month tour of every province in India to help end untouchability

    Kasturba Gandhi is arrested and imprisoned for the sixth time in two years

- 1944 Kasturba dies in detention at Aga Khan Palace at the age of 74

    After decline in health, Gandhi is released unconditionally from detention (this was his last imprisonment; he had spent 2338 days in jail during his lifetime).

- 1948 Gandhi is assassinated at Birla House by Nathuram Vinayak Godse

Group Activity

Browse History books and the internet and find out about the Indian freedom struggle. Collect information and make a project on it. Some of the points on which you could dwell are:
- Indian history and British colonial rule
- Exploitations of Indians at various levels
- Rise of the freedom struggle
- Role of a freedom fighter (especially Gandhi ji)
- Indian independence

Class Discussion

What is your idea of caste system in India? Discuss with your teacher in class. Which do you think is better—a class-ridden society or a class-less society? Give reasons for your answers.

Questions

1. Who was Mahatma Gandhi?
2. What is he well known for?
3. Where was he born?
4. Write briefly about his parents.
5. What kind of a boy was Gandhi in his youth?
6. Why do you think he followed the path of 'ahimsa'?

Activities

7. Name at least 3 Indian mythological characters by whom he was influenced.
8. How did Gandhi develop respect for all religions?
9. Write about an incident which talks about his honesty.
10. When did Gandhi get married and to whom?
11. How many children did they have?
12. Where did Gandhi study law?
13. Why was Gandhi horrorstruck in South Africa?
14. What did Gandhi do to abolish untouchability?
15. What was Gandhi's vision regarding women?
16. Write briefly about the Dandi March.
17. Who assassinated Gandhi?
18. Enumerate briefly his contribution to the betterment of pre-independent India.
19. Name a few international leaders who were inspired by him.
20. What do you learn from his biography?

Glossary

ahimsa: avoidance of violence towards others as found in Hindu, Buddhist and Jain traditions

ashram: a hermitage, monastic community

assassinate: murder of an important person

assimilation: the process of fully understanding some information or idea

beneficial: favourable or advantageous

bitterness: lack of sweetness

catalyst: a substance that increases the rate of a chemical reaction without undergoing any permanent chemical change itself

celibacy: the state of keeping oneself away from marriage

commitment: to be dedicated to a cause or activity

composite: made up of several parts or substances

comprehensive: dealing with all or nearly all elements of something

condolences: sympathy or compassion

constitution: a body of fundamental principles established for a state or other organization

cremate: to dispose a dead body by burning it

Glossary

to ashes mourning: expression of sorrow on a person's death

criticism: disapproval of someone or something

debates: a formal discussion on a particular matter in a public meeting in which opposing arguments are put forward

dedicated: devoted to a task or cause

depressed: a state of unhappiness

disclose: to make known

discrimination: the unjust treatment of different categories of people on the grounds of race, age, or sex

downtrodden: to be treated badly by people in power

dowry: property or money brought by a bride to her husband at the time of marriage

earnest: having sincerity

elementary: very basic

embarked: to go on board a ship or aircraft

embodiment: a tangible or visible form of something that is abstract

encourage: to give support and confidence

enlightenment: the action of attaining spiritual knowledge

enshrined: a place for a precious object in an appropriate holder

entourage: a group of people attending to an important person

established: to have existed for a long time

esteemed: to be respected and admired by all

fortunate: lucky

guardian: a person who protects or defends something

gymnastics: exercises displaying physical agility

Harijan: a member of a hereditary Hindu group of the lowest social and ritual status

headstrong: willful and determined

heartless: a complete lack of feeling

horrified: to fill with shock

ideology: ideas and ideals formed on the basis of economic or political theory

illegal: prohibited by law

immemorial: to extend beyond memory, record, or knowledge

Glossary

Glossary

immigrant: a person who comes to live permanently in another country

impressed: to feel admiration for someone

inferior: lower in rank

injustice: lack of fairness

inspiration: the process of being mentally stimulated to do or feel something

institution: an organization established for a religious, educational, professional, or social reason

jealous: feeling or showing an envious resentment of someone

massacre: brutal slaughter of many people

mediocre: not very good

nominate: to propose or formally enter as a candidate for election or for an award

opportunity: a set of circumstances that makes it possible to do something

Parsee: a follower of Zoroastrianism

passive: not active

perception: the power to become aware of something through the senses

permission: to officially allow someone to do a particular thing

prerequisite: a thing that is required as a prior condition for something else

principality: a state ruled by a prince

relentlessly: to do something in an unendingly intense manner

repentance: to be sorry for something

resistance: the refusal to accept something

restore: to bring back

rigorous: extremely thorough

riots: a violent disorder of peace by a crowd

sacrifice: an act of slaughtering an animal or person as an offering to a God or Goddess

satyagraha: passive political resistance, especially that advocated by Mahatma Gandhi against British rule in India

scolded: to rebuke someone angrily

scriptures: sacred writings of Christianity existing in the Bible

secularism: the principle of separation of the state from religious institutions

Glossary

segregation: to set someone or something apart from others

shackles: a ring or other fastening made of iron to bind the wrist or ankle

sovereignty: the supreme authority

squatting: to crouch or sit with knees bent

struggle: to make forceful or violent efforts to get free of bondage

subjugate: to bring under control

toil: to work extremely hard

tolerance: the ability to withstand something that one dislikes

unification: the process of being united

untouchability: not allowed to be touched or touch something

varna: each of the four Hindu castes Glossary

vegetarian: a person who does not eat meat or fish

violate: to fail to comply with a rule

widow: a lady who has lost her husband